Katrina: Our Side of the Story

**Past, Present, and Future of Bay Saint Louis & Waveland, Mississippi
as told by Middle School Students**

With a Foreword by Charles Gray of the Hancock County Historical Society

Nokia and the Nokia Connecting People logo are registered trademarks of Nokia Corporation

Printed in the United States of America

First edition 2006

Every reasonable effort has been made to verify the factual accuracy of the content of this book. The Bay Waveland School District and the Hancock County Historical Society accepts no responsibility for inaccuracies resulting from the anecdotal nature of the information provided.

10 9 8 7 6 5 4 3 2 1

Library of Congress Control Number: 2006931942

Book Design: Andrew Lewis, Ben Lewis, Seth Everts, Erik Gregory
Editing: Laurie Johnson, Trish Medalen
Production: Wendy Darling

Katrina: Our Side of the Story. Past, Present, and Future of Bay Saint Louis and Waveland, Mississippi as told by Middle School Students

ISBN 0-9772319-3-3

Pearson Foundation, New York 10019

www.pearsonfoundation.org

This book is dedicated to the young generation
facing the devastation of Hurricane Katrina.

The future of the Gulf Coast is in good hands.

Mobile
Learning
Institute

Special Thanks

This book is the result of hours of work on the part of Bay/Waveland Middle School students; Charles Gray and Eddie Coleman of the Hancock County Historical Society; Kim Stasney, Carolyn Barcelona, Sandra Reed, Angie DeFraites, and Gina Pepperman of the Bay/Waveland School District; Vannessa Nickson of Nokia; and Mark Nieker, Andy Lewis, Ben Lewis, Seth Everts, Erik Gregory, Kyla Thompson, Wendy Darling, Trish Medalen, and Laurie Johnson of the Pearson Foundation.

About the Images

The majority of photographs displayed in this book were taken by Bay/Waveland Middle School students, with additional shots by Erik Gregory, Andy Lewis, and Ben Lewis. Historical drawings, lithographs, and photographs appear courtesy of the Hancock County Historical Society.

About This Book

Published to coincide with the first anniversary of Hurricane Katrina, *Katrina: Our Side of the Story* documents a series of remarkable collaborations that took place in the first weeks and months following this devastating storm.

Beginning in September, 2005, representatives from Pearson – including members of Pearson Education, the Financial Times Group, the Penguin Group, and the Pearson Foundation – visited Bay Saint Louis and Waveland, Mississippi with the goal of helping the residents of these communities begin to recover from Hurricane Katrina. The Pearson community helped school officials welcome back students to temporary "tent school" structures and initially served as the school's sole temporary teachers. When school formally re-opened in November, Pearson stayed on and worked closely with teachers to assess student needs, providing personalized reading and math intervention that supported teachers' classroom instruction.

In January, the Pearson Foundation and Nokia together made their Mobile Learning Institute Digital Arts Residency program available to Bay Waveland School District students and teachers. Developed as a way to share the latest mobile phone and computer technologies in the classroom, this program makes it possible for young people to share their own ideas and stories of their experiences with each other, their teachers, and their families.

As might be expected, students were eager to share their individual experiences of Katrina, but they were also just as eager to work together to share all that had happened to their towns, and to share their thoughts and hopes for all that still needed to be rebuilt.

With the help of Charles Gray of the Hancock County Historical Society, students in Gina Pepperman's middle school classes researched life in the Mississippi Gulf Coast region before the storm. They then photographed and documented the specific damage of Hurricane Katrina on city buildings, businesses, and homes. Finally, they worked together with representatives from the Mobile Learning Institute to create brief digital films that shared all they'd discovered.

These remarkable films – each fully researched, written, and composed by Bay Waveland School District students – were shared with classmates, teachers, and families. Just as important, they have been donated to area libraries and archives as lasting documents of the impact of Hurricane Katrina on the region.

Now, with the publication of this book, the places, stories, and images that defined their towns can be shared again with Bay Saint Louis and Waveland residents. *Katrina: Our Side of the Story* will also introduce visitors to the wonderful people and places that continue to define and shape these communities.

Mark Nieker
President, Pearson Foundation

See the films whose stories and images
serve as the foundation for this book at
www.mobilelearninginstitute.org

CONTENTS

South Beach

Depot

Waveland

FOREWORD

CHARLES GRAY
Executive Director
Hancock County Historical Society

Charles works on the book with Andy Lewis and Ben Lewis.

Charles helps a student find pictures from his database.

The ends of eras are always bittersweet. So it was on August 25, 1699, when the Choctaw village of Chicapoua became the French Colonial village of Bay Saint Louis. Three hundred six years and four days later, on August 29, 2005, Hurricane Katrina laid waste to Bay Saint Louis and drastically changed the lives of those who lived here.

As we have searched among our ruins and gathered small pieces of our lives, we've been aware of the reactions of our fellow citizens to this great disaster. Some have risen bravely to the tasks of clearing and rebuilding, while others have retreated into the darkness of their fears or left the coast forever. It is with this in mind that we put together these thoughts and pictures assembled by Bay/Waveland Middle School students who shared with us their reactions to what has happened to them.

One must necessarily be proud of the younger generation's acceptance of their losses, their resilience in restarting their lives, and their very special insight about things that are really valuable. While some memories are intensely personal, like "memories at Grandmother's house" or specific teen hangouts that no longer exist, most reflect a more general view of life at the Bay. These young people seem to want the same atmosphere their parents and grandparents had. They want the town to closely resemble its pre-Katrina status. Change has not come easily to this coastline. Very old houses (one dating from 1787) were still being used as private homes, and some had been in the same families for more than 140 years. The beautiful bay and shoreline remain, as do most of the magnificent live oaks. The walk and bike path along the sand to Waveland is undisturbed, and families still stroll in the cool evening breezes until late at night.

Following are notes and pictures of places from the kids' memories; they are the places they have named as having been important to them.

INTRODUCTION

SANDRA REED
School Administrator
Bay/Waveland School District

Sandra's home in Long Beach, Mississippi before Katrina hit.

Sandra's home in Long Beach, Mississippi after Katrina hit.

On August 29, 2005, a girl named Katrina attempted to totally change life on the Mississippi Gulf Coast. If Hurricane Katrina thought for a second she might knock the wind (no pun intended) out of all the folks living along this coast, she had obviously never met the young teenage population in Bay Saint Louis and Waveland, Mississippi. To give the infamous storm her due, she did render almost all students in the Bay/Waveland School District homeless. However, she would need to blow much harder to render this bunch helpless.

In true GRITS (for all you non-Southerners, that would be *Guys/Girls Raised In The South*) fashion, the students of Bay/Waveland Middle School in Bay Saint Louis, Mississippi grieved for a short while and began the business of speedy recovery. While I'm sure their hearts vacillated among feelings of happy/sad/hopeful/hopeless/determination/fright, their faces always indicated a will to survive.

When students at Bay/Waveland Middle School were presented with an opportunity to document their Hurricane Katrina experiences utilizing the Mobile Learning Institute, they jumped at the opportunity. The result of the project is this book. It illustrates the many stops along their journeys to recovery – on both a physical and an emotional level. I offer sincere thanks to Nokia and the Pearson Foundation for helping our students along this path.

As the students roamed the community taking photographs, their thoughts and emotions were set free in a cleansing and healthy manner. To say the process was cathartic for the students would be quite the understatement. It's always been said that a picture speaks a thousand words, yet few students knew that taking a picture speaks many words, as well.

I'm proud of the compassion that our students extended to others during and after the storm. I'm proud of the way our students held their heads high in spite of losing every item owned by their families. I'm proud of the hard work our students devoted to documenting their Hurricane Katrina experience. HECK, I'm just plain proud of our students.

Enjoy, and please never feel sorry for or pity our students, despite the circumstances they have been dealt. Celebrate the fact that they were given an opportunity to grow; more importantly, celebrate the fact that they accepted the challenge and are part of rebuilding their home – the Mississippi Gulf Coast.

TEACHER'S NOTE

GINA PEPPERMAN
Eighth-Grade Teacher
Bay/Waveland Middle School

Two of Gina's students interview a Katrina victim at his FEMA trailer.

CAROLYN BARCELONA
Principal
Bay/Waveland Middle School

"While this school year is not like any other, I can still take great pride in the achievements of our school community and our community as a whole. We have survived such devastation, yet still accomplished things that seemed unimaginable, and we have done this together. I ask that students and parents honor the generosity that has been extended to our school."

This digital arts residency has been a wonderful experience for my students. The Mobile Learning Institute has been extremely helpful. Its instructors taught my students to use digital cameras and how to take interesting photographs. The classes then went into our storm-ridden area and took photographs of sights that are way too familiar. This was an emotional experience for all of us, resulting in powerful movies created by the kids that convey their experiences during Katrina. In turn, those movies were the source for the book you now hold in your hands.

Once we gathered our photos and interviews, we then went to the Historical Society and gathered before-the-storm shots and historical information. Finally, with the assistance of Erik Gregory and Kyla Thompson from the Mobile Learning Institute, students wrote and recorded their stories.

The student stories have brought many tears to all who have watched the movies. Children their age should never know so much heartache and destruction. This project was such a meaningful event for everyone involved. As a teacher, I feel that this has helped many of my students cope with the craziness that surrounds them.

Students are now beginning to see that there is hope and that we will get through this. We are glad that we had this opportunity to share our stories with everyone. We hope you see that we may have been down, but we are not out. Our youth will aid our recovery and will help our community to come back to life.

Thank you to Nokia and the Pearson Foundation for allowing my students a chance to have their voices heard and enabling them to begin the healing process. Hurricane Katrina is an event that no one will forget; but for my 65 students, this book, too, will never be forgotten, because it brought them hope and a much needed sense of closure.

NORTH BEACH

"This was the first time I saw a drawbridge!"
Jon, 6th grade

*"I used to eat at Trapani's with my family.
They had really good seafood."*
Alex, 7th grade

"I used to pick up the Sea Coast Echo
newspaper for my mom."
Savannah, 7th grade

SECTION ONE

This was my home.

Brandon & Katelyn

"Once you have visited here, you will understand why it was so hard to lose everything."

Jonathan & Brandon

"Hurricane Katrina left a great devastation to the Gulf Coast, but perhaps in time, it can be a wonderful place again."

Brett & DaParis

"We just want things to get back to normal again."

Meggie

"I took these pictures to show how beautiful the houses were. Some were historical houses and need to be remembered instead of being a pile of trash. In the future, I really hope that these houses will be rebuilt to look the same way they did before Katrina."

Ashley & Chad

"Even though Bay Saint Louis was destroyed, we hope that someday it will be better than it was before."

Matt & Chase

"I am thankful for all the people who have left their homes to come down and help us rebuild. We did not even have to ask them to come. They say that they just want to help us, which makes us feel really good."

Pete Fountain's House

Pete Fountain is a local musician who became well known throughout the United States. He is descended from a very old family in the Gulf. The Fountain family dates back to the Fountaine Caddy family, for whom Bayou Caddy is known. Pete's great-grandmother was Celeste Favre, an Indian maiden wife of Simian Favre. Brett Favre, the legendary NFL quarterback, is also descended from Celeste. Pete Fountain's home was a handsome, broad house with long low galleries. It had quite extensive acreage, sat back very naturally under the oaks, and offered lovely perspectives from every angle.

To find out more about **Pete Fountain's House**, see the movie made by **Meggie** at www.mobilelearninginstitute.org/katrinastories.htm

Elmwood Plantation

One of the great losses in Katrina was Elmwood Plantation. Elmwood was built on an original French land grant. In 1804, Jesse Cowan purchased the house and continued building. The result was a West Indies plantation house, with large, heavy columns on the ground floor and smaller, turned columns on the second floor.   The ballast brick used to build the house was shipped from France. There were enormous hand carved beams in the ceiling and the attic. The house was surrounded by grand oak trees. Jesse Cowan and his family owned the plantation for many years. During the Civil War, Mr. Cowan went off to fight, as did his sons. After Mrs. Cowan died, the house was ransacked, and everything in it was stolen or hauled away. When the boys returned from the war, they camped in the house overnight, and then went on to New Orleans. They went into business for several decades, until the great fire of Julius Street burned them out. At that time, they again returned to Bay Saint Louis, occupying and starting reconstruction on the house. For two centuries, the house was recognized as one of the finest pieces of architecture in southern Mississippi, almost totally unaltered since 1804. It had 18-inch-thick walls throughout the building. When the wave of Katrina hit it, the house became a pile of rubble, no more than 15 inches tall.

To find out more about the area near **Elmwood**
see the movie made by **Jonathan and Brandon** at
www.mobilelearninginstitute.org/katrinastories.htm

Bay-Waveland Yacht Club
Bay St. Louis, Mississippi

Ray Stieffel
Bay St. Louis, Mississippi

"When I was younger I remember the Yacht Club being the first place I learned how to use a sailboat."

Madeline, 10th grade

Yacht Club

In the 1800s, Bay Saint Louis was considered the playground for New Orleans, as New Orleans has no beaches. (To the south it has only swamps, bayous, and waterways.) New Orleanians came to the Mississippi Gulf Coast for their weekends. Subsequently, the Bay-Waveland Yacht Club was formed in 1896. The club's first building was destroyed in a 1915 hurricane. The Yacht Club purchased the Big E's Grocery building, where it stayed until the depression forced the club's closure. In 1948, the club regrouped and purchased the property on which it currently resides. Many of the boats were destroyed as a result of Hurricane Katrina.

To find out more about the **Yacht Club**
see the movie made by **Jonathan and Brandon** at
www.mobilelearninginstitute.org/katrinastories.htm

Bay Bridge

U.S. 90 Bridge-Bay St. Louis, MISS.

The first bridge across the Bay of Saint Louis was built in the mid-1800s out of creosote-coated timbers. When the local summer temperature reached into the 90s, the creosote was virtually boiling, and very often melted. Many people crossing the bridge would throw out cigarettes, which caused repeated fires. Often, the bridge would be closed for several days. There is a story of a local man and his girlfriend who came across the bridge from a nearby city one Saturday evening, to watch a movie. While they were here the bridge burned, and he didn't get his girlfriend home until 2:00 in the morning. He states that as the reason they are married today! The new bridge proposal brings the height up to 80 feet, which will allow boats to pass under it.

To find out more about the area near **the Bay Bridge** see the movie made by **Matt and Chase** at www.mobilelearninginstitute.org/katrinastories.htm

Monet-Breath House

Along the Mississippi Gulf Coast, houses are titled with the original owner's name, followed by the current owner's name, with a hyphen between them. Judge Monet of Bay Saint Louis originally owned the Monet-Breath House. The house was built in 1814, and began as a Creole cottage. In 1809, the owners built a turret on the left end of the room they call the North Wing. The bedroom to the north side (left side in pictures) was built around 1890. Under the house there is a French fort built out of brick. It has slotted gun windows facing out to the beach. The door to the rear on the southwest corner has an offset wall to avoid arrows attacking through the open door. There was originally a fantastic oak tree in front of the house that had a large hollow in it. Children could climb through the hole in the center of the tree and have a full-size room in which to play. One child built a fire in it, and set the tree on fire and enlarged the hole through the center of it. At one point it was like a great chimney still standing in good condition. During the Civil War, the family hid their gold, silver, and other valuables in the tree and planted ferns in front of the hole to hide the contents. Hurricane Katrina damaged the special tree, and it has since died.

To find out more about **The Monet-Breath House**, see the movie made by **Meggie** at www.mobilelearninginstitute.org/katrinastories.htm

St. Augustine's Seminary

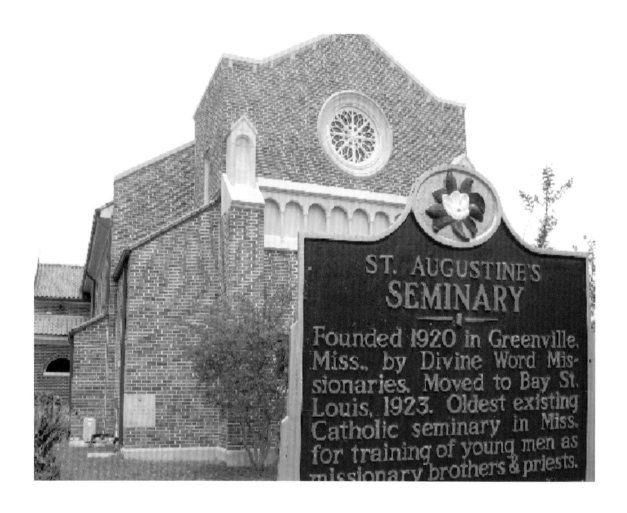

Saint Augustine's Seminary was founded in 1920 and has been in continuous operation ever since. It is the oldest existing Catholic seminary in Mississippi. It was also the first seminary in America for black priests. It is no longer a teaching school, but is used as a recreation and retreat destination for priests. The seminary still has 27 acres, with a beautiful grotto on the grounds.

To find out more about **St. Augustine's Seminary**, see the movie made by **Ashley and Chad** at www.mobilelearninginstitute.org/katrinastories.htm

Bay Town Inn

The de Montluzins built the house in 1900 on the site of an old French fort. It had sleeping accommodations for seventeen people. The house withstood the hurricanes of 1915 and 1947, and sustained only roof damage from Hurricane Camille in 1969. Shortly thereafter, the family sold the house. It was then converted into the Bay Town Inn. When Katrina hit, the owner spent several hours in the tree in front of her inn and was forced to watch as the storm destroyed everything around her.

To find out more about **The Bay Town Inn**, see the movie made by **Brett** at www.mobilelearninginstitute.org/katrinastories.htm

The Bay Saint Louis Little Theatre was established in a living room in 1945. A group of citizens banded together to form a new cultural niche for artistic residents. The group's first production was "The Twelve Pound Look." It was performed at the local high school auditorium. The group then moved to a temporary wooden building in another part of town. In 1948, the board of directors purchased a plot of land and assembled a more permanent building. The building was originally made from two war-surplus army barracks.

To find out more about **The Little Theatre**, see the movie made by **Brett** at
www.mobilelearninginstitute.org/katrinastories.htm

Sea Coast Echo

The *Sea Coast Echo* newspaper dates back to June of 1892. There were earlier papers in the area, but most of the information came from the Pass Christian newspaper. The original newspaper office was in the building at the 100 block of North Beach Boulevard. That building was constructed in 1900 to replace the building across the street, which had been on pilings out over the water. Former employees have said that every time the presses started, the building rocked so violently that people fled from it, fearing that the building was going to fall. The newspaper has missed only two issues in its entire history. Both days were following hurricanes when it was physically impossible to get them out. After Hurricane Katrina, publication began immediately from the dining room of an employee. The paper was carried away and printed, then brought back for distribution.

To find out more about the area near **The Sea Coast Echo**, see the movie made by **Brett** at www.mobilelearninginstitute.org/katrinastories.htm

A&G Theatre

The A&G Theatre first opened its doors in April of 1927. Miss Ames and Mrs. Gaspard (A&G) had the new fireproof structure built on the site of their home. It had a seating capacity of 1,000, and cost over $60,000 to build. The A&G was directly across the street from their previous theater (erected in 1915), which in turn had replaced an even earlier theater built in 1905. The first theater was an open-air platform with bleachers along the sides. It was called a "nickelodeon," as admission was five cents.

To find out more about **The Old Theater**,
see the movie made by **Brett** at
www.mobilelearninginstitute.org/katrinastories.htm

Trapani's

The Trapani's location that was destroyed by Katrina had been in existence for only a few years before the hurricane hit; but Trapani's has been a staple of the area for decades. During the McCarthy inquiries, the door was locked to avoid complications with the law. In order to get in, you knocked on the door and recited a "knock-knock" joke. That signaled that you were a friend, and they would open the door and let you in. Knock-knock jokes became the key to entering the Trapani restaurant-emporium. In 1969, it was completely destroyed in Hurricane Camille. Trapani's opened again in Waveland on Highway 90; a business that is still running, and is known as Trapani's Knock Knock. Trapani's is a tremendously popular establishment that is always crowded – a favorite with both locals and visitors.

To find out more about **Trapani's**, see the movie made by **Brett** at www.mobilelearninginstitute.org/katrinastories.htm

"*Before the storm, I used to watch*
The Krewe of Real People *parade.*"

Zach, 9th grade

"*The restaurants in Old Town were awesome. They were the best places to get food.*"

Rachael, 6th grade

"*The shops in Old Town used to be good places to hang out.*"

Adele, 7th grade

"*We always went and had fun at the Old Town parades.*"

EJ, 9th grade

My town is still alive.

Daron & Greg

"Five months after the storm everything still looked fresh."

Kim & Leann

"We have lived here all of our lives, and have seen something so terrible come and destroy all of it. Bay Saint Louis was always open to others, and was never trashy until Katrina hit."

Main Street Methodist Church

The Main Street Methodist Church was built in 1895. In the late 1800s, a local man donated the grounds for the Main Street Methodist Church. In 1892, his son subsequently donated the adjacent property, to be used for the parsonage. Both men served as mayors of Bay Saint Louis. For more than a century, the church has been a centerpiece of Old Town. During Hurricane Katrina, the prominent steeple was blown across the street.

To find out more about **The Methodist Church**, see the movie made by **Kim and Leann** at www.mobilelearninginstitute.org/katrinastories.htm

DO NOT REMOVE STEEPLE

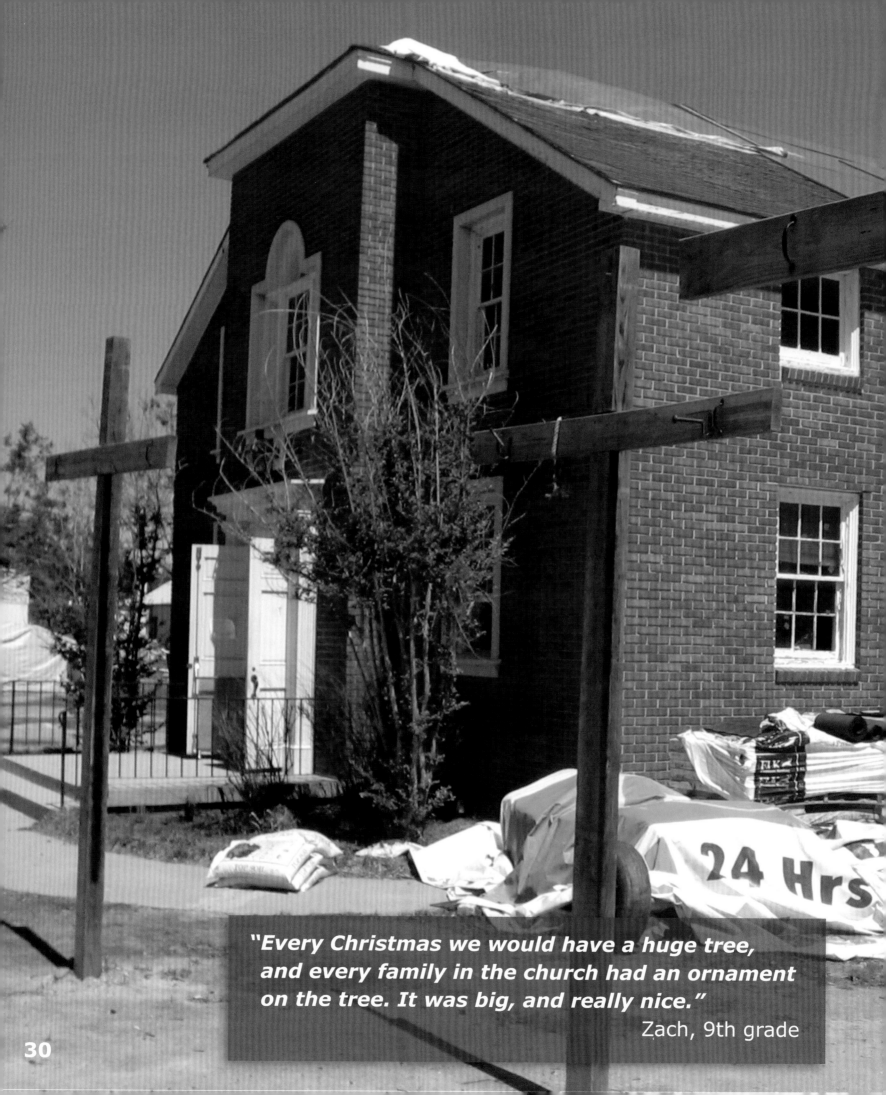

"*Every Christmas we would have a huge tree, and every family in the church had an ornament on the tree. It was big, and really nice.*"

Zach, 9th grade

First Baptist Church

The First Baptist building was renovated from a surplus army chapel, which was brought across the bay after World War II. It featured exposed beams and siding from the old barracks. The church was established in 1896, and has roots traceable to 1846. That church lot was purchased in 1895 for $75. The original property was then sold to the city, and is now a cemetery. The church has endured many hurricanes and fires; in 1977, a major fire forced the church members to rebuild the sanctuary. The sanctuary is still in use after Katrina, with an ever-resilient congregation.

To find out more about **The First Baptist Church**, see the movie made by **Kim and Leann** at www.mobilelearninginstitute.org/katrinastories.htm

Courthouse

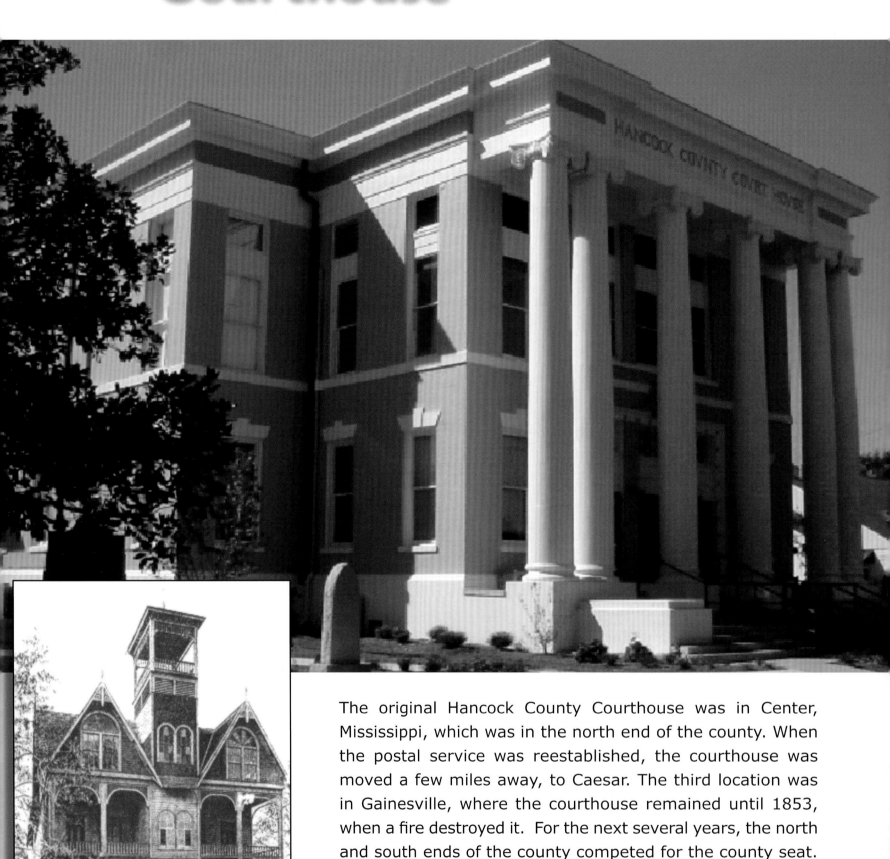

The original Hancock County Courthouse was in Center, Mississippi, which was in the north end of the county. When the postal service was reestablished, the courthouse was moved a few miles away, to Caesar. The third location was in Gainesville, where the courthouse remained until 1853, when a fire destroyed it. For the next several years, the north and south ends of the county competed for the county seat.

To find out more about **The Courthouse**, see the movie made by **Daron and Greg** at www.mobilelearninginstitute.org/katrinastories.htm

In the 1870s, the county seat was moved to Bay Saint Louis. Court was held in the Old Spanish Customs House until a courthouse building was constructed on the 200 block of Main Street. A larger courthouse was then built on the site of the present building. The current courthouse was built in its place in 1810, and opened in 1811. It is a beautiful, great revival building. It originally had a cupola on top, which blew off in 1969 during Hurricane Camille. The current building was severely damaged in Katrina, but there are plans to restore it and return it to court use.

HANCOCK COUNTY COURT HOUSE, BAY SAINT LOUIS, MISS.

Ruth's Cakery

The bakery was originally constructed as a commercial building in the 1940s. Ruth Thompson, a New Orleanian with Gulf Coast ties, moved to the city and opened her first bakery in one of the shopping centers. Due to the extremely high rents where she was, she selected the current location on Court Street. When Ruth opened, she baked everything from donuts and cinnamon rolls to various pastries. It soon became the center of social gatherings. She provided free coffee, had a large gathering room, and even housed the Hancock Historical Society. Due to physical restraints, she has specialized in making the finest wedding cakes in the Gulf. She changed the name of the business from Ruth's Bakery to Ruth's Cakery, and she is considered by many to be one of the great decorators of the current time. The building was badly damaged in Katrina, and Ruth says that she is going to reopen in a smaller building to primarily make her famous wedding cakes.

To find out more about the area near **Ruth's Cakery**, see the movie made by **Kim and Leann** at www.mobilelearninginstitute.org/katrinastories.htm

"Before Katrina, we used to go down to the beach and play volleyball after school."

Zach, 9th grade

"*Before the storm, for the Fourth of July, my family and I would go down to the beach to light off fireworks.*"

Savannah, 7th grade

"*Da Beach House bonfires, on Friday nights, were always a lot of fun.*"

Jon, 6th grade

"*Big E's had the best snowballs!*"

Adele & Rachael, 7th grade

The beach was beautiful.

Kahla & Gabby

"Mississippi is a devastated state and we would like y'all to help us."

Cody & Glenn

"We hope Bay Saint Louis will come back together even stronger than it was."

Patrick & Mikey

"For the future of Bay Saint Louis, we would like it to be a very cozy home town with many family businesses. No matter what it looks like, we will always be proud of our hometown."

Jennifer & Jacob

"Some people are lucky they actually have a home to come home to."

Heather & Jessica

"We really liked Bay Saint Louis the way it was before the storm. We are hopeful it will come back."

Ashley & Carly

"Waveland and Bay Saint Louis were truly great places to be. They were places full of excitement and energy."

Cynthia & Britany

"Instead of pews, we now have to sit on lawn chairs."

Devin & Demitry

"We hope they rebuild the Bay Saint Louis beach front to look just like it did before Katrina."

This is my home.

Jonathan & Nathaniel

"At the end of our journey, we saw something we will never forget. There was a single flower growing among all the destruction. We felt it telling us that Bay Saint Louis is coming back, and hopefully it will stay."

Dustin & Ryan

"It may not look like much, but even the smallest bit of growth is a miracle for us. "

Brennan & Jarrod

"In the next ten years we hope Bay St. Louis and Waveland are at least back to normal, and maybe even better."

Hancock Bank

Hancock Bank was founded in 1899. It is rumored that the bank began with two barrels and 10,000 dollars. The rent at the original location was seven dollars a month. The Hancock Bank is now one of the strongest banks in America. The current structure was built on the site of the old Levy's department store that closed in 1898. Immediately behind it was the jailhouse, where Hancock Insurance, another part of the Hancock Corporation, now resides.

To find out more about **Hancock Bank**,
see the movie made by **Dustin and Ryan** at
www.mobilelearninginstitute.org/katrinastories.htm

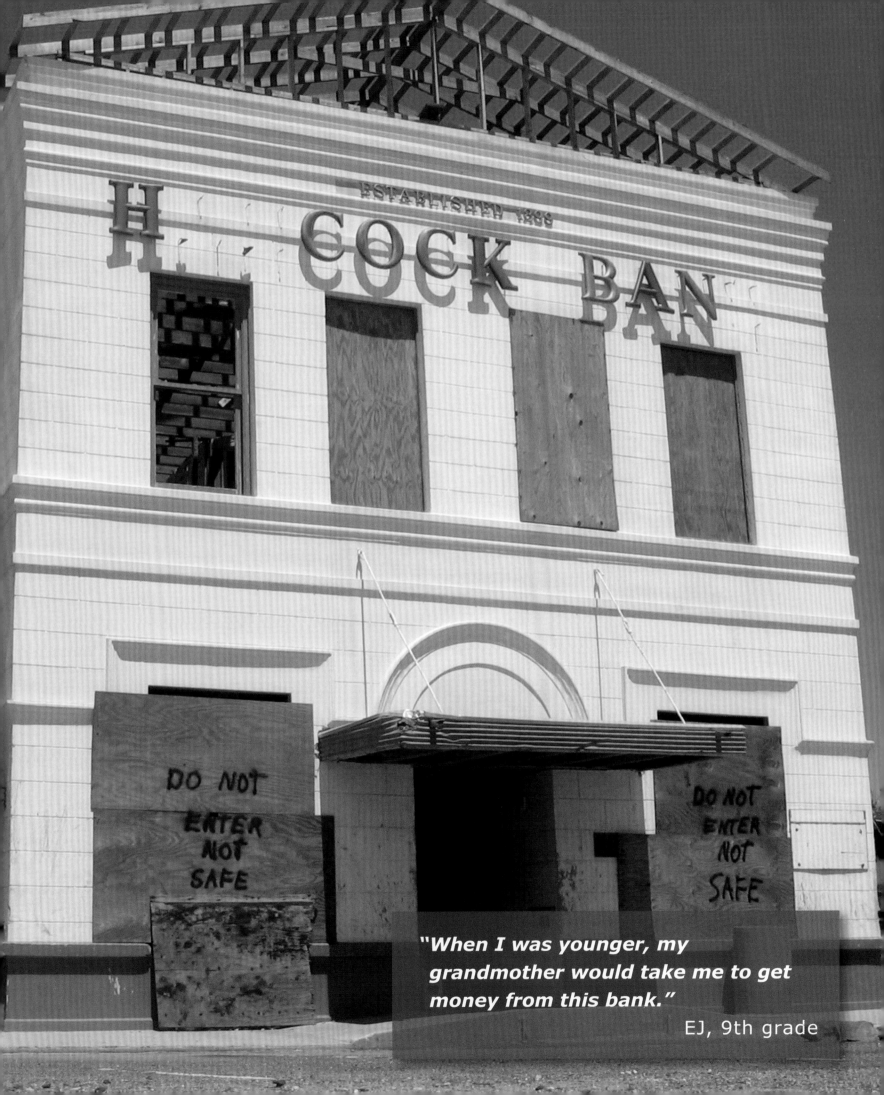

ESTABLISHED 1899

H COCK BAN

DO NOT ENTER NOT SAFE

DO NOT ENTER NOT SAFE

"When I was younger, my grandmother would take me to get money from this bank."

EJ, 9th grade

JEAN BAPTISTE LE MOYNE
SIEUR DE BIENVILLE (1680-1767)

EXPLORED THE BAY OF SAINT LOUIS
ON AUGUST 25, 1699 AND NAMED IT FOR
LOUIS IX OF FRANCE

Tercentenary Park

On August 25, 1699, a group of French explorers stumbled into Bay Saint Louis on a hunting expedition. Bay Saint Louis citizens consider this date to be the origination of the city. Jean Baptiste le Moyne d'Bienville is credited with establishing the town, in honor of France. Tercentenary Park was created to honor the 300th anniversary of that date. With a large financial gift from the CEO of the Hancock Bank, and help from the Historical Society, the city celebrated the opening of the park on August 25, 1999. The statue of Bienville, along with the 100 year-old palm tree, withstood Hurricane Katrina. The park occupies a small lot directly west of the Hancock Bank.

To find out more about **Tercentenary Park**, see the movie made by **Brett** at www.mobilelearninginstitute.org/katrinastories.htm

47

St. Stanislaus College

St. Stanislaus College, Bay St. Louis, Miss.

The Brothers of the Sacred Heart established St. Stanislaus College Preparatory in 1854. It has an international reputation of excellence in both academics and sports. The beautiful thirty-acre campus supports an impressive array of sports activities, which has earned many honors for the school. It has an average enrollment of 600 students, with about half of the students living on campus.

To find out more about **St. Stanislaus College,** see the movie made by **Brennan and Jarrod** at www.mobilelearninginstitute.org/katrinastories.htm

Our Lady of The Gulf

Our Lady of the Gulf Catholic Church was founded on August 8, 1847, when Father Buteaux arrived in Bay Saint Louis. The new church was blessed and completed in 1849, and services have been held ever since. The beautiful Gothic style building burned in 1907, and the present building was completed the following year. It has exquisite stained glass windows which were made in Munich, Germany. Each window depicts an event in the lives of Jesus, Mary and Joseph, from the Annunciation to the Resurrection of Christ.

To find out more about **Our Lady of the Gulf**, see the movie made by **Cynthia and Britany** at www.mobilelearninginstitute.org/katrinastories.htm

Big E's

Elvis Keller established the Big E building as a grocery store in 1894. It was a very beautiful brick building with arched front windows. After Elvis Keller's death it become the Bay Waveland Yacht club. The Bay Waveland Yacht club had originally occupied space on a pier, but was washed away. The Yacht Club purchased Big E's around 1925. When the Yacht club later moved, Big E's became a movie theater, and then again a local grocery store. During Hurricane Katrina, the residents of the building escaped to the roof of the shed behind it. They managed to commandeer a boat and go to dry land from there. Devastatingly, one of the residents was not able to survive the storm, and drowned that day.

To find out more about **Big E's**, see the movie made by **Kahla and Gabby** at www.mobilelearninginstitute.org/katrinastories.htm

Da Beach House

Da Beach House was originally part of the adjacent Big E Grocery. It was an Oldsmobile dealership with large glass windows across the front of it. After being closed for a short while, it was renovated into a Hawaiian themed coffee shop and rental store. In a culture that was not usually so colorful, it was very successful. The people of Bay Saint Louis loved and enjoyed it as a popular place to hold parties. The store had kayaks and bicycles for rent, and served various coffees. Many times at sunset, the owner would come running around the building wearing a Hawaiian outfit and carrying a torch in order to light the torches in front of the building. Da Beach House was host to local music productions and various speakers, including Stephen Ambrose and Charles Gray.

To find out more about **Da Beach House**, see the movie made by **Kahla and Gabby** at www.mobilelearninginstitute.org/katrinastories.htm

"*When I was younger, I used to say that when I had a car, I would drive every morning and get a smoothie from Da Beach House.*"

Zach, 9th grade

Old Spanish Customs House

Hancock County boasted the largest sawmill in the world until June of 1930. The houses in the Bay, with minimal exception, were built out of heart pine or cypress lumber. The Old Spanish Customs House was built in 1787. The bricks that were used were baked on site with the date baked into them. There were two buildings of note that were built out of brick: The Elmwood Plantation, and the Old Spanish Customs House. Bay Saint Louis has no native clay suitable for making bricks. The clay was brought in baskets, and the bricks were molded and fired.

There is no verification that it was ever actually an official customs house. The official customs house was on the second floor above Levy's department store, which is now the Hancock Bank. The only potential connection is a customs agent who lived in the Old Spanish Customs House. It was a typical house of that period, consisting of two floors. There were three rooms on each floor, a large room in the center with a gallery that completely surrounded it, and a single gable roof over the entire house. It was spectacularly simple and elegant, and was a private home at the time of its Katrina destruction.

 To find out more about **The Old Spanish Customs House**, see the movie made by **Jonathan and Brandon** at www.mobilelearninginstitute.org/ katrinastories.htm

Coast Episcopal Church

Coast Episcopal Church was originally a beautiful little wooden church in a different location in Bay Saint Louis. In 1905, Charles Sanger was paid 500 dollars to move it down 2nd street, where it stood from 1905 until 1969, when Hurricane Camille completely devastated the building. Rather than building back on the small corner lot, the congregation purchased property on South Beach Boulevard. Katrina completely leveled the South Beach Boulevard building except for the bell tower, which is still partially intact today.

To find out more about **Coast Episcopal Church**, see the movie made by **Brandon and Anthony** at www.mobilelearninginstitute.org/katrinastories.htm

DEPOT

"Me and my little cousin got stopped by the police when we would play on the railroad tracks."

EJ, 9th grade

"Benigno's was a lot of fun, and the the food was really good."

Alex, 7th grade

"When I was little, my mom worked at the train depot. I remember visiting her at work."

Jon, 6th grade

SECTION FOUR

I see my future.

Zach & Harry

"Katrina was a very powerful and destructive storm. This town will never be the same."

Jordan & Brianna

"We want Bay Saint Louis to be bigger and better than before. We want all the places in Bay Saint Louis to come back. We love Bay Saint Louis, Mississippi."

Old Town Depot

The railroad was completed in June of 1870, and immediately a row of businesses sprung up across from the depot. This became the center of the downtown business district for three decades, until the turn of the century. There were grocery stores, hotels, bars, and liquor stores. The current selection of stores includes many popular restaurants and bars. The families who own the Benigno's Grocery and Deli and Benigno's Bar are still in business in the area, more than one hundred twenty years later.

To find out more about **The Depot**, see the movie made by **Harry and Zach** at www.mobilelearninginstitute.org/katrinastories.htm

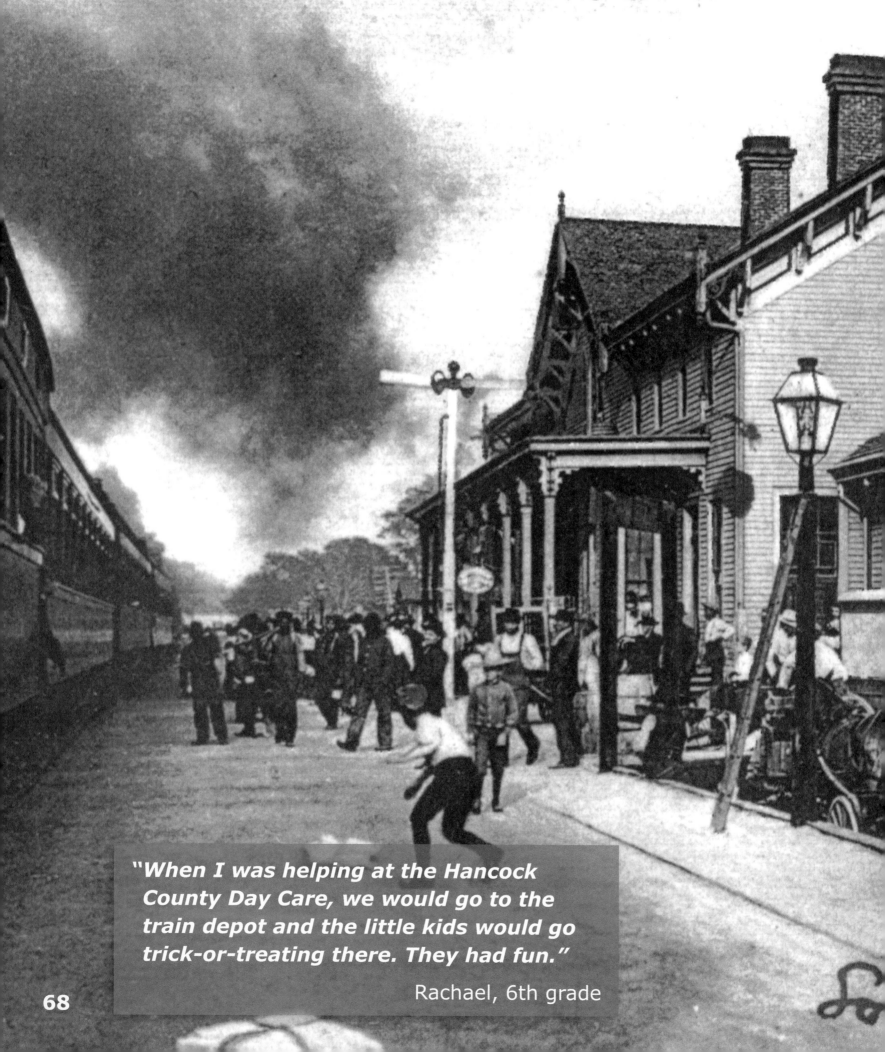

L. & N. R. R. Station, Bay St. Louis, Miss.

"*When I was helping at the Hancock County Day Care, we would go to the train depot and the little kids would go trick-or-treating there. They had fun.*"

Rachael, 6th grade

L & N Depot

The train depot building was constructed in 1928. The previous building was in considerably bad shape. The citizens of Bay Saint Louis repeatedly petitioned the train company for a new building. The only response they received was a letter stating that the company did not think a new building was needed. That very weekend, the building was destroyed in a fire. The new depot was built within a year, and became the hub of the developing business community. After Hurricane Katrina, the depot once again became the center of operations for Bay Saint Louis. This included a medical center, temporary City Hall, and many other essential operations for the crippled city.

To find out more about **The L & N Depot**, see the movie made by **Harry and Zach** at www.mobilelearninginstitute.org/katrinastories.htm

Scafide House

In 1965, *This Property is Condemned* was filmed using the depot, Old Town, and the Scafide Home and Store as the backdrop. The movie starred Natalie Wood, Robert Redford, Charles Bronson, and Alan Baxter. The story was based on a Tennessee Williams one-act play of the same name. The Scafide House was the movie's home for the character played by Natalie Wood.

This Property is Condemned

Originally, the house was a private residency, as well as a store. John Scafide built the house in 1929, personally casting all the stones. Mr. Scafide was a well-known Tulane football player nicknamed "Baby Grand." He also served as the mayor of Bay Saint Louis.

To find out more about **The Scafide House**, see the movie made by **Harry and Zach** at www.mobilelearninginst org/katrinastories.htm

St. Rose Church

St. Rose de Lima (Peru) Church is dedicated to the first saint of the Americas. Father Henry LeDug, of Our Lady of the Gulf Church, began a school for black children in 1868. St. Rose de Lima Catholic Church was built in 1926 as an outgrowth of the school. The congregation had become too large to meet in the school chapel, so the St. Rose church was built. In recent times, the church has enjoyed a regional reputation for being full of life and joy.

To find out more about the area near **St. Rose Church**, see the movie made by **Harry and Zach** at www.mobilelearninginstitute.org/katrinastories.htm

Alice
Moseley

Folk Art
& Antique

MUSEUM

"*Before she died , I got to meet her.
She was a nice lady, and she did
beautiful paintings.*"

Alex, 7th grade

Alice Moseley

Alice Moseley, already an elderly lady, once visited a Bay Saint Louis art show and fell immediately in love with the town. She drove back to north Mississippi and got her cat. She returned to Bay Saint Louis, sent for her things, and lived the rest of her life on Union Street. She bought a little front-and-side-galleried shotgun cottage, which she promptly painted a strong blue. One of her best-known paintings is titled "The House May Be Blue But the Old Lady Ain't." Her paintings were an immediate success all over the Gulf Coast. At the time of her death, there were contracts for any pieces she had ever painted. Since that time, her son, Timothy Moseley, has opened her home as a small museum and sells prints of her paintings.

To find out more about the area near **Alice Moseley's House**, see the movie made by **Harry and Zach** at www.mobilelearninginstitute.org/katrinastories.htm

WAVELAND

"*I liked Waveland because it was green and had lots of shade. Most of the trees are gone now because of the storm.*"

Savannah, 7th grade

"*It used to look a lot better than it does now. You had to watch out for the jellyfish, though.*"

Barabino, 8th grade

"*Buccaneer Park had the coolest wave pool.*"

Madeline, 10th grade

Our lives have changed forever.

Haleigh & Courtney

"Getting around town isn't easy. Signs are all torn up or crooked."

Zach & Josh

"You just can't even believe it unless you see it for yourself. Luckily, many people are stepping up to the challenge of rebuilding."

Rainee & Lyndi

"Hopefully, the city and beach will turn out the same way as it was before the storm, because it was the dream city to live in."

Atilla

"The area used to be full of people and jobs; it was really lively. Now it is just depressing."

Chelsea & Amanda

"Nothing is the same. There are only a few places to eat or shop."

Anthony & Brandon

"As we sat in the park and looked at the devastating aftermath of the storm, we both wondered what we will do in the summer to beat the heat."

We still need tons of help.

Heidi & Keionda

"We would like Bay Saint Louis and Waveland to stay the same. We would like the same businesses and the same features as they had before."

Rachel & Megan

"In the future, we would like to have street signs, and sewers that don't leak."

Paul & Chris

"No one could have predicted this kind of disaster, and the storm has changed the lives of many people."

Danica

"I hope Bay Saint Louis and Waveland will remain a bedroom community, and keep away from a lot of advertising and duplexes."

Austa & Sarah

"Houses were destroyed and signs blown down, and everybody's stuff was in their yards. Katrina was the worst storm ever. It destroyed everything in its path, took lives and caused problems for everyone."

Deja View

The house known as Deja View was a relatively new house, built in the last decade. The original family home was called Twin Pines. It belonged to the Hemail family and was washed away in Hurricane Camille. The builders of the recent version of the house styled it after Mediterranean architecture they had seen on a trip. Ironically, the Deja View was designed to withstand a category five hurricane.

To find out more about **The Deja View**, see the movie made by **Danica** at www.mobilelearninginstitute.org/katrinastories.htm

Jean Lafitte

The house known as the Pirate House, or Jean Lafitte's house, was a Greek revival house built around 1803. Whether Jean Lafitte actually built it, or the man who ran Lafitte's financial businesses out of New Orleans did, is not known. Lafitte was usually on the run from somebody or another. Lafitte robbed ships and came and went. He appeared in Bay Saint Louis, New Orleans, and many unknown places in between. The house was one of the prettiest houses ever built on the Gulf Coast. There are strong rumors around the Gulf that the house had a dungeon and tunnels. The most prevalent rumor says there was a main tunnel leading forward from the house, under the sand beach, and came up in a sand island offshore. No map shows any such sand island.

At the time of the Battle of New Orleans in 1815, Jean Lafitte gathered his men and joined Andrew Jackson in defense of New Orleans at Chalmette. For this service he was absolved of all of his crimes, was made an American citizen again, and was free to travel. Lafitte could not be good very long, and shortly thereafter he wound up in trouble in Galveston, Texas. He was run out of the state, went to the Yucatan, and lived a few years. His death was reported in 1825. There is, however, a deed in the Hancock County Courthouse that he and his wife signed in 1826, 11 months later than his recorded death. NASA has sounded his grave in the Yucatan and he's not in it. The death in the Yucatan was most probably faked. Rumors persist that he came back to the Bay of Saint Louis and lived to be a quite old man, incognito, simply as a former soldier who fought at the Battle of Chalmette.

To find out more about **The Jean Lafitte House**, see the movie made by **Paul and Chris** at www.mobilelearninginstitute.org/katrinastories.htm

St. Clare Church and School

St. Clare was the first Catholic church in Waveland. St. Clare now hosts a prestigious elementary school, with an enrollment of about 200 students. The students are now meeting in donated tents. Even with the church building completely destroyed, the spirit of the congregation is strong, and the hope is to rebuild St. Clare.

To find out more about **St. Clare Catholic Church**, see the movie made by **Danica** at www.mobilelearninginstitute. org/katrinastories.htm

"*That is where all our family reunions were before the storm. We would play ball and go to the wave pool, but after the storm we can't now.*"

EJ, 9th grade

Buccaneer Park

Buccaneer Park is the site of the old Andrew Jackson house. The area was a popular getaway location for many pirates in the 1700s. It is prominently featured in many of the mysterious tales of buried treasure and looting. Until the storm, Buccaneer Park was a very popular family establishment. Many high school students from Bay Saint Louis and Waveland worked at Buccaneer Park.

Andrew Jackson's House

At the very south end of Beach Boulevard, below Waveland, is Bayou Caddy. It's the end of all roadways headed southwest toward New Orleans. From there, travel is only by kayaks and boats. Just before the bank of Bayou Caddy there is a high ridge that runs east to west, known as Jackson Ridge. In 1803, Andrew Jackson purchased a house on this property. Shortly thereafter, the house had a severe fire and the Jacksons rebuilt. Mrs. Rachel Jackson died just seven days before Andrew went into the White House as President. His daughter-in-law, Sarah, served as First Lady for the United States. After the presidential years were over, Sarah came to the house and lived in it. She named the house "Seasong." It was quite large at this point – 92 feet across each side with galleries totally surrounding it. Mrs. Jackson hated the house because it was so secluded.

It took seven or eight hours by carriage to get to Bay Saint Louis. One had to follow the ridge west out to the Pearl River to go around the swamps, go north, then come in through the prairie land to get here. Rachel's son, Samuel, and his wife also lived at Seasong for many years. The Jackson family eventually lost the plantation in bankruptcy, and the house burned down in 1937. The government took over the area and opened Buccaneer Park.

To find out more about **Buccaneer Park and Andrew Jackson's House**, see the movie made by **Brandon and Anthony** at www.mobilelearninginstitute.org/katrinastories.htm